115 Ways

to

Reduce Anxiety

Strategies for Dealing with an Anxiety Disorder

By Mike Marcoe

115 Ways to Reduce Anxiety

10-Digit ISBN 1-59113-872-8
13-Digit ISBN 978-1-59113-872-3

Printed in the United States of America.

Booklocker.com, Inc.
2006

DISCLAIMER

This book provides content related to topics about weight loss, nutrition and health. As such, use of this book implies your acceptance of this disclaimer.

About the Author

Mike Marcoe is a writer and editor from Middleton, Wisconsin. He has been writing about money and investing issues for years. Additionally, he has worked as an editor of social science texts and personal finance articles. For paper copies of this book, please contact Mike Marcoe at **mgmarcoe@yahoo.com** or via **www.mikemarcoe.com**.

Contents

Introduction

From "Learn a Martial Art" to "Restructure Your Thinking," *115 Ways to Reduce Anxiety* will give you valuable suggestions for treating anxiety, whether it is specific or general.

The tips offered here have been studied and researched by both scientists and therapists, and many are well-known parts of anxiety-therapy plans. Some come from the medical field, and others come from nutritional, physical fitness, and even spiritual approaches.

Many of the ways, such as practicing breathing exercises, will look familiar. Others, such as studying philosophy and eating whole grain foods, may look new and unfamiliar. They all attack anxiety symptoms from different angles. Many are very

About the Author

Mike Marcoe, a long-time anxiety sufferer, is a writer and editor from Middleton, Wisconsin. He has worked for the University of Wisconsin–Extension as well as the financial education sector, social science, and various fiction markets. The author has also worked as a chef, bookkeeper, and newspaper deliveryman. He has participated in several anxiety therapies.

helpful to some people, while other methods may not apply to them. However, many people find that combining several approaches works best for them.

Anxiety disorders are the most common of all mental disorders. Contrary to popular belief, anxiety is not the same thing as stress—instead, it is the result of one's natural anxiety mechanism gone awry. Reducing it can be quick, or it can take a long time of repeated practice; consider creating an action plan as suggested at the end of this book to ease into any changes you implement.

Anxiety reduction is a lifelong process for some people, and it comes with learning new sets of skills and outlooks on both yourself and life. I hope you find many useful ideas in the following chapters to create an enduring set of changes in your life.

Note: the ideas presented in this book are suggestions. They have been found by anxiety sufferers to work. The author makes no guarantee that they will work for you. Author takes no responsibility for any adverse effects experienced by any readers.

Section 1

Identify Your Anxiety First

Distinguish Between Normal Anxiety and a Disorder

As you begin to cope with your anxiety, you must do one thing:

1) Know the difference between an anxiety disorder and regular anxiety.

Anxiety is a state of apprehension that results when we anticipate a real or imagined, but unknown, danger. Anxiety is necessary: it serves to keep us safe from danger. But when the symptoms exist in the absence of real danger, then anxiety turns into a disorder: it takes on a life of its own and does not serve its original function. At this point, it is wise to consider professional help, because the disorder will interfere with your life functioning.

There are several forms of anxiety, so it is good to consult a doctor or other reputable source to examine your symptoms. Not all forms of anxiety produce the classic symptoms of jitteriness and other physiological excesses. Sometimes symptoms are purely cognitive. Medical and psychological manuals like the *Diagnostic and Statistical*

Manual of Mental Disorders (DSM) offer diagnostic criteria for true disorders. If you meet enough of them, you may need to seek professional help for your anxiety. If you don't, home therapy may be all you need unless your symptoms are interfering with your ability to function.

Symptoms of an anxiety disorder include the following (consult the DSM for additional symptoms):

- In the case of phobias, avoidance of the feared situation or object
- Symptoms last at least six months
- Symptoms interfere with a person's normal functioning
- Symptoms are not caused by a medical disorder or by any ingested substances
- Muscle tension
- Excessive worry
- Difficulty in controlling worry
- Restlessness or irritability
- Sleep disturbance
- Concentration difficulties

> **Note**
>
> Distinguishing between normal anxiety and an anxiety disorder often requires the help of a doctor or other trained therapist. Once you distinguish between them, you can begin to create a plan to treat yourself.

- Physical/sexual difficulties
- Significant personal distress
- Persistent sense of dread
- Heart palpitations
- Dizziness
- Excessive worry
- Racing thoughts

Know Which Forms of Anxiety Apply to You

2) *To design an effective treatment plan, you need to know which type of anxiety you have.*

Otherwise, you may not make much progress, as some treatments are applicable only to certain types. Often, you can easily recognize the different types.

Which types of anxiety apply to you?

Generalized anxiety disorder. This is anxiety without a clear reason. There is no specific fear or reason for the anxiety. You are in a state of constant worry and tension, always expecting some kind of catastrophe to happen. This kind of anxiety can be difficult to treat, as it is usually not connected to any specific stimulus.

Phobias. These are very specific fears. Examples are fear of heights, water, tight spaces, cats, public speaking, etc. In many cases, they can lead the sufferer to change their living habits. One of the most incapacitating phobias is agoraphobia, the fear of public places. People with this phobia may actually avoid going outside.

Panic disorders. These are more severe than phobias and generalized anxiety. Panic attacks develop quickly and last for a matter of minutes. The trigger may not be identifiable.

Obsessive-compulsive disorder. This well-known disorder involves persistent, obsessive thoughts along with persistent, compulsive behavior used to deal with those thoughts. OCD sufferers use rigid, ritualistic behavior and may repeat actions dozens of times each day.

> **Note**
>
> *3) Narrow your anxiety down to the types you actually have, as this action will help to reduce it. This works because once you know the extent of your anxiety, you feel in control of a larger part of your mental universe.*

Post-traumatic stress disorder. PTSD is a reaction to an event of extreme stressfulness. The person may be emotionally numb or emotionally heightened, or both at different times.

Each of these classes breaks down into several subgroups. Some sufferers have overlapping symptoms as well. For example, people with generalized anxiety frequently suffer from obsessions.

Section 2

❧

Using Your Mind

Challenge Your Fears

4) Prove that you have anxiety or fear.

Often, anxieties arise from delusions—for example, the deep, unconscious belief that a person cannot measure up in some area. As a method of treatment, a therapist may ask the person to prove that belief. In most cases, the fear is not supported by reality. (But in some cases, it is! When this happens, a treatment plan is designed for it.) The therapist's challenge may sound scary, but it has been shown to work.

Much anxiety is built on faulty perceptions that originally had some basis in reality but got distorted. Eventually, these perceptions can become self-fulfilling, which is why you should examine them and determine whether or not they are accurate. This challenge may be easier with phobias because they're easier to isolate—they occur only in specific situations.

5) Write down all your fears.

Be as specific as possible. This will help you narrow down the amount of your mental space that is taken up by fears. It will also help you see where your anxiety ends and your strengths begin. Then write down a way to challenge these fears. After that, try out the challenge.

You may be surprised by what you find. Below is an example of such a list.

To challenge this:	Do this:
"Everything is falling apart."	6) *Find specific examples of things that are falling apart in your life. Make a list. It will not be infinite. Then make a list of things that are not falling apart.*
"I have a phobia about speaking to people."	7) *Speak in different scenarios, such as on the phone, in a supervisor's office, etc. Learn that not all social situations provoke anxiety.*
"I can't do this task. It's too overwhelming."	8) *Break up tasks into parts. Then see whether you can do them.*

The goal is to narrow down your list of things that cause your anxiety. Eventually, you will learn that there are fewer causes of your phobias than you thought. As you realize that you have control over your life, the occurrence of your symptoms may become less frequent.

Many cognitive therapists are trained in helping clients do exercises like these.

Restructure Your Thinking

Hearing "It's all in your head" may not help you much, but the way we think does affect our mental health. It may help to remember the famous quote by Epictetus, the Greek philosopher: "People are disturbed not by things but by the views that they take of them." Studies of successful people find that they do not practice self-defeating thinking. They like challenge, and they:

9)   *See anxiety as a natural part of life.*

They view it as a part of their lives, something to work with, rather than something to avoid at all costs. They have internal control over their lives and do not see themselves as victims. Therefore,

10) *Do not see yourself as a victim.*

Successful people do not interpret failure as the end of the world. Many anxiety-prone people, on the other hand, have what is called an *external* locus of control, meaning that they feel outside forces are dictating their choices and actions. They also have a sense that everything is about to "fall apart." They frequently ruminate excessively on this notion, despite a lack of evidence. Such a mindset can be changed by changing one's thinking.

Identify as many illogical, unreal, self-defeating thoughts as you can. This process will take a long time as you plumb the depths of your mind for them. Then counter each one with a healthy, realistic alternative. Below is the beginning of such a list:

If you are thinking:	Then do this:
It's all over.	11) *Think "I failed in this one attempt. I will try it another way. Maybe another way will work."*
I am an anxiety-ridden person.	12) *Think "I have anxiety in only certain areas of my life, not in all of them."*
I am completely nonfunctional.	13) *Think "Only certain areas of my self aren't working well, such as (for example) self-esteem and social functioning."*
I must have only the highest expectations of myself at all times.	14) *Think "High expectations do not work at all times. Only realistic expectations work."*

Your goal is ultimately to see things as they really, truly are. Once you do, you may find your anxiety easier to handle. Your anxiety may go away. Try keeping a journal of your thinking patterns. Also, ask friends if they notice any unhealthy thought patterns in you. You may discover some surprises.

Quote

I had an appointment with a psychiatrist to deal with panic attacks while driving. I crossed the Willamette River on an errand (near downtown Portland, Oregon), but for some reason could not drive across a bridge to come home. I was really freaked out. I've also had this problem on windy roads in mountain passes.

I called and cancelled the day of the appointment: September 12, 2001, because all of a sudden MY problems just didn't matter anymore. I haven't had an attack since.

Jenny
Portland, Oregon

See the Limitations of Black and White Reasoning

Black and white thinking does not leave room for adaptability, which is needed to cope with any kind of change or threat. Instead, such thinking allows the person to feel safe for a short period of time. This kind of mindset can contribute to problems like depression and anxiety because it ultimately makes the person feel helpless to change. This form of thinking, also called "all-or-none" thinking, is well known in therapeutic circles. Are you a black-and-white thinker? If so, perhaps you think using words like the following:

- Always
- Never
- Disaster
- Perfect
- Only
- Completely
- Failure
- Can't be done

If these words describe you, then:

> 15) *Try "gray" thinking instead. This thinking is realistic because it takes the nuances of experience into account.*

Although black-and-white thinking is correct and necessary at certain times, the anxiety-ridden person uses it even when it is not (and sometimes, *especially* when it is not). At these times, realistic thinking is useful. Here are some examples.

Black and white	To be realistic, think:
I have low self-esteem.	16) *I have low self-esteem only in some areas.*
There is only one right way to do things.	17) *There are several right ways to do things.*
I'm too intelligent to have done something so stupid.	18) *Even intelligent people can do stupid things.*
This has to be perfect. Otherwise, it can't possibly work.	19) *Most things can work with imperfections in them, or perfection takes time.*

Study Philosophy

There's more to philosophy than sitting on a rock in deep thought, or arguing abstract ideas that do not apply to real life. Philosophy was created to deal with real life. It improves our ability to think clearly and objectively. It roots out thinking patterns that are based on unexamined beliefs. Because of these benefits, you may find it helpful in treating your own anxiety.

Philosophy is routinely used in cognitive psychology, the branch that explores how we think. Very often, unhealthy, unrealistic thinking patterns exacerbate anxiety, stress, and phobias. Philosophy develops realistic thinking.

Philosophy is broader than cognitive psychology—it helps you uncover and understand broad truths about life, which may treat anxieties.

How to use philosophy to reduce anxiety

20) *Examine beliefs that may be creating or worsening anxiety.*
21) *Identify thinking patterns you thought you believed in but really didn't.*
22) *Examine anxiety-causing beliefs that **do** have a basis in reality!*

Where do you start reading?

Try reading an introductory philosophy text, such as *The Story of Philosophy* by Will Durant, or *Philosophy for Dummies* by Tom Morris. Most libraries carry a few of these entry-level books. Such a book will cover most aspects of humankind's philosophical accomplishments. Be sure to check out philosophies from around the world as well, along with works from under-represented groups (they can often point out flaws in another culture's accepted thinking). As you undertake your studies:

23) *Watch for certain themes that jump out at you.*

If you find yourself returning to them over and over, you will find these especially helpful to your own concerns. They may be key to your anxiety situation.

24) *Take a course in logic.*

Logic streamlines your thinking and roots out forms of reasoning that are contradictory or otherwise not based on coherent foundations. During and after you have taken such a course, you may find yourself persistently examining every statement under the sun, whether yours or someone else's!

Don't Try to Be So Perfect

Many anxiety-prone people suffer from perfectionism. If you are one of them, perhaps you:

- Persistently obsess about how something could have been done "perfectly."
- Spend an abnormally large amount of time thinking about flaws—any flaws, on anyone, anything, anywhere, and in any time.
- Can't work unless everything is in perfect order.
- Can't like something or someone unless it fits a seemingly endless list of requirements.
- Are so afraid to fail you don't even want to try or finish something.

If you are this kind of person, there are steps you can take to reduce your own perfectionism and, eventually, your anxiety. You need to start small.

25) Look for the beauty in imperfect things.

For example, notice how people with imperfections or disabilities manage to carry on with their lives.

21

26) *Note all your small successes. Write them down in a journal.*

27) *Add up all the tasks you have put off doing for perfectionistic reasons.*

Then compare them to the number of small, seemingly meaningless tasks you have done.

28) *Deliberately do some things imperfectly, just so you can monitor how you feel about them.*

Try this at home when no one is watching. Then make the necessary corrections. Often, anxiety sufferers follow strictly regimented courses of action because they feel they can maintain control that way.

29) *Break up long tasks into small ones that do not provoke any perfectionistic anxiety.*

30) *Practice active awareness on how your perfectionistic thinking arises, occurs, and goes away.*

Note how it makes you feel afterward.

31) *Stop thinking, "Such and such went well, but …"*

The goal is not to embrace sloppiness or to lower your standards, but to be realistic. When you are realistic, you can actually get *more* done and feel better about your accomplishments.

If all else fails, you can see a therapist who specializes in anxiety treatment. He or she can give you more specific strategies for combating perfectionism.

Note

Perfectionists don't want perfection for perfection's sake. Instead, they want always to be *not good enough*. That way, they don't have to put forth the kind of effort that could arouse anxiety. Perfectionism is a way to keep performance anxiety away. It forever keeps the person from (a) facing anxiety and (b) working to their full potential.

Are You an Approval Junkie?

Approval junkies are those who tie their self-worth to the approval of others. Not having the approval of others creates a state of anxiety in which they do things not for the joy of doing them, but to make others happy. Approval junkies try to "medicate" themselves and others with their own actions. Without the approval of others, they experience a general anxiety about life and their own worth. Approval junkies view themselves as flawed on a structural level.

This behavior is a recipe for unhappy living. If you are one of these people, your need for approval may be contributing to your anxious personality.

What can you do to combat an unhealthy need for approval?

32) Learn to do things for your own benefit.

If the joy of doing things usually diminishes after a while, or you sense that something is a little off when you achieve success, your motivation may be wrong.

33) *Find out the motivations behind other people's criticisms of you.*

Are those people qualified? Are they biased? Are they criticizing you as a person rather than critiquing something you did or something you believe?

34) *Recognize that other people's approval can be valuable but cannot be the basis of your happiness.*

> Self-actualized people can live and work entirely for others, but their sense of self-worth does not come from this behavior.

Other people don't control how you feel. They can't—they don't have your mind.

35) *Take an inventory of all your strengths and develop them.*

Your talents are the key to developing a strong sense of self; a strong self never requires the approval of others for its own happiness and fulfillment.

36) *Learn that your self-worth is never dependent on what you do, but who you are as a person.*

Your growth as a person, however, will depend in part on your ability and willingness to achieve according to your abilities.

Not every approval-seeker is aware of this part of their nature. You may need to spend a lot of time examining yourself and how you feel about the things you accomplish.

Assert Yourself

Are you afraid to assert yourself? When you do, do you feel anxious? If so, your anxiety may be tied to your inability to assert yourself. In fact, *your anxiety may be a neurotic substitute for it.* Because emotions well up in situations that call for assertiveness, an inability to express them that way may result in you unconsciously substituting anxiety instead.

People who suffer from anxieties and phobias are often afraid to be assertive, and often they find out in therapy that learning to assert themselves lessens their symptoms. Many of them grew up in families that exhibited traits such as:

- Rigid family structure
- Overprotective parents
- Rigid belief system
- Performance-based acceptance
- Substance abuse
- Childhood abuse

Here are some tips for asserting yourself:

37) *Identify exactly what you really want/need, down to the detail.*

38) *During confrontation, describe the problem situation to the other person.*

39) *During confrontation, state how you feel. Be descriptive.*

40) *State the effect that someone's negative behavior is having on you.*

41) *During confrontation, state what you want.*

    Be positive about it: "I value your help, but I would prefer that you ask first before you give it."

42) *Use "I" statements to put the focus on what you want: e.g., "I want you to clean up this mess."*

43) *Avoid attacking the other person's character.*

    Besides being good for communication, this also helps reduce judgmentalism, which can contribute to black-and-white thinking.

44) *Use specifics instead of sweeping generalizations.*

    For example, don't say, "You never wash the dishes." Try saying, "I have noticed that you haven't done your part in washing the dishes for the past three weeks."

These methods of asserting yourself are ways to combat anxiety, as they are grounded in realistic thinking.

The Power of Genuine Emotions

Do you find it difficult to feel or express your own emotions, especially the negative ones? If so, you have company, because this trait is common in people with anxiety. In many of them, the anxiety substitutes for the emotions. When these people learn how to let themselves feel their emotions, their anxiety subsides.

Why do people not let themselves feel their emotions?

- Emotions can make some people feel that they are not in control of themselves.
- They may fear disapproval from others.
- Because they can be messy, emotions may make a person feel less than perfect.
- Emotions are clues to what we really believe about ourselves, other people, and life in general.

Many of the emotionally repressed are not even aware of it. They may see themselves as "in control," "neutral," "cool, "collected," "stress-free," or some other description that actually masks a kind of emotional flatness. These people often resist therapy because they see nothing wrong with themselves. It is only when they suffer a crisis involving a painful burst of emotions that they start to realize they are emotionally repressed.

45) *Examine how insistent you are that you are "cool," "neutral," or "in control."*

Two tips for learning to feel emotions:

46) *Identify any strong physical symptoms that occur when you are having negative thoughts. They may be a clue that what you are truly feeling is not being expressed or felt.*

47) *Notice the way people react to you. Their reactions can pinpoint what you are feeling.*

Once you can identify an emotion, you can better express it.

> **Note**
>
> As a general rule, anxiety is incompatible with strong, healthy emotions. They cannot exist together.

48) *Start expressing emotions with people you are comfortable with.*

49) *You may also want to consult a therapist who specializes in emotional therapy.*

Section 3

❡

Physical Approaches

Learn a Martial Art

The ability to defend oneself breeds a kind of mental poise that others notice. But martial arts go beyond that. They help you cope with neuroses like anxiety. Therefore:

50) Learn a martial art.

Martial arts, more so than regular exercise, work by generating power from one's own body. They do this by combining proper posture, breathing (both of which are confidence-instillers), and alignment of body parts. The result is a force greater than the sum of its parts; this is the famous "chi" energy that kung fu and tai chi practitioners cultivate. Through years of practice, a person learns to develop this power and use it to overcome attackers. He or she takes this power and controls it, using it for defense purposes.

Martial arts can also instill in you an internal locus of control, meaning an internally felt ability to control your life.

When a person learns to develop, access, and use power from within, anxiety naturally lessens. The effects can even be felt during the very first class.

Some people find that their anxieties (or various other issues) surface while they are sparring with opponents. This is normal. It just means that anxieties are coming to the surface of your mind, where they can be faced and dealt with. Many martial arts teachers are well aware of this phenomenon and can help.

When used correctly, the martial arts inspire *less* willingness to use violence. The confidence that is gained fuels assertiveness and an ability to stand up for oneself, and fighting becomes truly a last resort.

Tip

Attend a variety of martial arts schools at first. Many will offer a free introductory lesson. Also, watch educational videos on various self-defense methods and martial arts. Then settle on the art that works best with your body and about which you are the most enthusiastic. This will be the one that helps you the most.

Do Repetitive Activities

What do people do when they are stuck on a problem, or are so beset by worries that they can't think straight? They go for a walk!

Why? Because walking is repetitive. Repetition has a way of calming the nerves. Children know this instinctively. One of the ways that shamans and other practitioners of ancient religions enter trances is to repeat certain activities (sometimes to the point of boredom): widely spaced drumbeats are among the most common methods. When practiced regularly, repetition can also reduce generalized anxiety. People who pray regularly, or who knit regularly, or who walk regularly, know how their minds are freed from unnecessary worry when they do these tasks. With that in mind:

51) Make room for repetitive activities in your life.

What can they do for you?

- They train your mind to not expect results right away.
- They help you experience your own imperfections in a safe manner.
- They calm you down physically.

- They put you into a light meditative state, which releases your creative thinking.

- They free your ability to brainstorm.

- They remove your inner "critic" and thus free you from the constraints you may typically put on yourself.

The last three points above are partly why so many artists, writers, and actors work as waiters and waitresses; aside from the good money, the patterned work that they do is conducive to the creative mindset.

Here are some repetitive activities to do:

52) *Walk every day, usually on the same route.*

53) *Bike or walk to and from work every day.*

54) *Knit or sew, or do some other artistic activity, even if it's something easy, like paint by number.*

55) *Do some chore, such as dishes, on a regular basis.*

Exercise Consistently

The effects of exercise on mental and emotional health are well known. We've all heard of runner's high—that euphoric state brought on by endorphins. Exercise is also useful for treating anxiety symptoms.

A healthy, well-toned body handles the effects of nervous problems more effectively than an unhealthy one. Besides decreasing physical tension, consistent exercise helps you handle anxiety by increasing:

- Resistance to disease
- Endurance, which enables the body to withstand anxiety symptoms
- Emotional endurance
- Relaxation

What kind of exercise appeals to you?

56) Do aerobic exercise.

This is very good for combating anxiety symptoms. Try at least half an hour of aerobic movement three times a week, moving up to six or seven days over time. Most experts agree that three days are the minimum effective amount.

57) Take up weight training.

The resistance training from weights helps develop self-confidence and physical endurance.

58) Learn tai chi.

Tai chi is actually kung fu done in slow motion. It teaches you balance, poise, bodily control, and endurance, all of which can work against anxiety.

59) Learn dancing.

In addition to being great fun, dancing teaches poise, balance, and endurance, all of which help you withstand the effects of anxiety.

60) Try water exercise.

Water exercise promotes relaxation because of the motion of water.

As mentioned earlier, walk regularly, too. Walking provides a sustained, but lighter, aerobic workout. It also keeps the body toned.

If you are new to regular exercise or haven't done it for a long time, a physical checkup is recommended before you begin any exercise regimen.

Breathe

We all know what happens when we get anxious—we breathe quickly and shallowly. Those who have anxiety all the time become terrible breathers, and the inefficient breathing only compounds the problem. It increases both the pulse and the blood pressure. It can make it difficult for you to think clearly. The antidote? Learn to breathe deeply.

Deep breathing is often the fastest way to relieve the symptoms of anxiety.

Anxiety's physical symptoms are unpleasant and often frightening. The treatment for these symptoms will benefit the body and may also help alleviate mental and spiritual symptoms. Regular breathing exercises will help in all these areas. What's more, they will create for you an automatic calming response—the opposite of the fight or flight response. With practice, you can actually make yourself calm. Anxiety cannot exist in the presence of true calm.

How does a calming response treat anxiety symptoms?

- It uses less oxygen than is required in anxious situations.

- Breathing and heart rate slow down.
- Blood pressure and muscle tension decrease.
- It creates a sense of calm.

There are two main types of therapeutic breathing, and thus two approaches:

61) *Learn natural breathing.*

This means breathing from the abdomen. This is the way you should breathe all the time, except during strenuous situations. Try this for short periods each day until it becomes natural to you.

62) *Learn deep breathing.*

This means breathing first from your abdomen and then from your chest. It is a full, deep breath. Hold it for three seconds and exhale slowly. Try this at least ten times a day, but do not breathe this way all day long. This method is meant to train you for times when anxiety is present.

If you practice these regularly, you will learn how to naturally and automatically induce calm in anxious situations.

Work Outdoors

If you have ever tended a garden, you may know the sense of well being you get from it. It's not just the satisfaction of a job well done; there's something about being outside that is calming—perhaps because humans have spent the vast majority of their biological history outside, in natural light and fresh air. Modern life has removed much of what is natural. For those who suffer from generalized anxiety, doing outdoor work on a fairly consistent basis may provide relief.

For starters, it provides exercise and endurance training, which in themselves treat anxiety. Further, the human brain is habituated to natural sounds, such as birds singing, waves crashing, and trees swaying. These bring relaxation.

63) *Acclimate yourself to the sounds of nature. These sounds have rhythms that contribute to a reduction in anxiety symptoms.*

Also, attractive surroundings lower stress.

64) *Get plenty of sunlight every day, provided you are not restricted for medical reasons.*

Sunlight helps the body produce vitamin D, which enables the body to use calcium, a natural relaxant.

Touching plants and dirt brings a sense of connection to the earth and its bounty. For the religious, it may also connect one to the beauty of creation. Much of generalized anxiety disorder is tied to separation from what is natural. Therefore:

65) *Learn how to get dirty!*

Most of us work indoors, so fitting in some labor out in the elements may be difficult. Here are some ideas to try:

66) *Get involved in community gardening in your city. For a small yearly fee, you can have access to a plot of land all your own.*

67) *Volunteer with a state, national, or county park to do outdoor tasks.*

68) *Do landscaping or other outdoor work for a volunteer agency.*

Provided that precautions against temperature, excessive sun exposure, and natural pests are taken, you may find that working your body and mind outside goes a long way toward treating your symptoms and your underlying disorder.

Section 4

❧

Dietary Approaches

Eat Well

What we eat affects more than just our bodies. If you eat a well-balanced diet, you may notice some positive effects on your anxiety symptoms. Perhaps certain favorite foods may put you in a relaxed mood (alcohol excluded). For example, some people feel their nerves calm when they eat bananas— bananas have high levels of potassium, a natural relaxant.

Many nutrients are already known to counter anxiety. They include:

- Vitamin B1 (thiamine)
- Vitamin B2 (riboflavin)
- Vitamin B3 (niacin)
- Vitamin B6 (pyridoxine)
- Vitamin B9 (folic acid)
- Vitamin C
- Vitamin E
- Calcium
- Chromium
- Magnesium
- Omega 3 fatty acid
- Potassium
- Tryptophan

A list of the foods that contain these nutrients is too long to list here. However, a diet rich in dark green, leafy vegetables, fresh fruits, whole grains, nuts, beans, and moderate amounts of meat and dairy will provide all of them.

Here are some more tips for using nutrition to treat anxiety:

69) *Eat foods that contain several nutrients in one.*

   Beans and dark green leafy vegetables are great sources of several nutrient groups.

70) *Substitute traditional foods with similar, but nutrient-packed, foods (like spinach for iceberg lettuce).*

71) *Get your nutrients in their natural state.*

   Unlike vitamins, natural sources have additional nutrients not found in pill form, such as disease-fighting compounds.

72) *Work on making a regular practice of eating well.*

   This will help condition a regular relaxed state for you. Learn cooking if you must. Many people will not admit it, but natural, nutritious food actually tastes much better than processed food and junk food. After all, it was designed to. You will discover this if you persist at it.

Eat Whole Grains

Complex carbohydrates are useful tranquilizers. They increase the amount of serotonin in the brain, thereby inducing relaxation. Their benefits are only reaped, however, when you consume these carbohydrates in their whole-grain form. If you do not already eat whole grain foods, consider doing so. They are one of nature's own anti-anxiety medications.

When grains are refined, only the starch remains. From your stomach, this starch rushes into the bloodstream, raising the blood sugar and then dropping it quickly. Low blood sugar can create symptoms of anxiety, such as trembling, dizziness, sweating, panic attacks, fatigue, confusion, nervousness, etc. (For some people, high blood sugar also creates anxiety.) Whole-grain foods are absorbed much more slowly, because the fiber slows the flow of starch into the blood.

Refining grain strips it of its bran and germ to make it last longer on shelves (the oils in the germ would go rancid after a while if they were not removed). The remaining starch is enriched with B vitamins and some minerals, but several more vitamins and minerals and almost all phytochemicals (natural disease-fighting substances) are not replaced.

73) *Substitute whole-grain alternatives for your white breads, rice, and pastas.*

If you experience a taste shock, try substituting gradually. Examples of whole grain foods include:

- Brown rice
- Unhulled barley
- Whole-grain pasta
- Bulgur wheat
- Whole-wheat pizza
- Whole-grain oats
- Many cereals
- Whole-wheat burger and hot dog buns
- Whole-wheat pancake and biscuit mixes
- Whole-grain, non-wheat pastas

If you are sensitive to food, you may notice positive effects very shortly after eating. Unfortunately, few restaurants offer whole-grain food items at this time.

Get Rid of Sugar and Stimulants

Everyone knows caffeine makes people jittery. Research has shown that consuming a lot of caffeine can exacerbate anxiety. In some people, symptoms drop noticeably after they stop consuming caffeine.

74) Reduce your caffeine intake for a few weeks to see whether it works for you.

Beyond this, try getting your starches from complex carbohydrates, rather than sugar, and make sure to get them in whole-grain form. As explained in the previous chapter, low blood sugar can create anxiety symptoms. Eat more whole grain foods to combat this.

If you consume	Try this instead
Caffeine	75) *Drink green tea or chamomile tea. Chamomile is a known reducer of anxiety symptoms.*
Sugary cereal	76) *Eat whole-grain cereals.*

Sugary drinks	77) Pair sugary drinks with a protein source, like peanuts.*
Candy bars or other sugary snacks	78) Eat whole-grain chips. These products improve in quality every year.

To begin, note all the sources of sugar and stimulants in your diet. Where possible, substitute them with something else. Healthy snacks have come a long way in the last few years, and there are now many tasty options.

Cutting out (or down on) sugar or stimulants may feel like an uphill battle, but if you suspect that your symptoms are related to them, the reward will be worth it.

* Protein slows the rate at which sugar enters your bloodstream, thus reducing eventual low blood sugar.

Herbal Remedies

Herbs have long been used to treat anxiety symptoms. You may already be familiar with how kava kava or a cup of chamomile calms nerves.

> *79) Try anxiety-reducing herbs, as teas, baths, tinctures, lotions, and/or capsules.*

They may work on neurotransmitters in the brain, or they may affect the outward symptoms of anxiety, such as muscle tension.

Herbs can also have negative side effects, especially if taken in large doses or if you are already taking other medications. Also, anxiety herbs in liquid form may have alcohol in them, which can cause headaches.

Always consult a physician before using herbs as a treatment program or for a prolonged period. This is especially true if you already use other medications.

Herbs commonly used for anxiety

- Catnip
- Chamomile
- Fennel

- Feverfew
- Hops
- Kava kava
- Mullein
- Oats
- Passionflower
- Sage
- St. John's Wort
- Valerian (the source of valium)

If you experience generalized anxiety, try a variety of herbs. Be sure to study them thoroughly first, and if you have any concerns, ask a medical professional.

Avoid Dehydration

Some people notice that adequate water intake produces a calm mind and body. This is not an accident: dehydration can cause anxiety, as well as dizziness, cramps, and compromised coordination. Over seventy percent of the brain is water, and when we don't drink enough, the body suffers.

Water is the most important substance we consume. It keeps the body and brain running optimally. Adequate water intake also helps distribute nutrients throughout the body. Many of these nutrients, like calcium and B vitamins, also treat anxiety symptoms.

Nutritionists recommend eight cups of water a day. By "cup," they mean the volume measurement, not the container. Be sure to measure the volume of your glasses and bottles. Most actually hold more than a cup.

One good idea is to fill up two or three containers every morning with your required water for the day (usually 64 ounces). That way you can monitor your water intake.

Try these ideas:

80) Get most of your water early in the day.

You may be able to feel positive effects if you start your day with two or three cups of water for breakfast. Drink another two at lunch, then two at dinner, and the rest between meals. This may take a lot of practice for some people.

81) *If you can't get most of your water early in the day, try getting into the habit of drinking enough water for each meal.*

This may help to keep your symptoms at bay all day long.

82) *Cut down on alcohol. The resulting dehydration may trigger your symptoms.*

Also, the depressant action of alcohol can make you physically anxious, and it will require you to drink even more water.

83) *Eat foods that naturally contain a lot of water.*

One good example is leaf lettuce. Besides being watery, lettuce is a well-known anti-anxiety herb.

84) *Keep water in your car, at your desk, in your locker, in your backpack, and in other places.*

As the single most important substance you consume, it is important to have water available at all times.

85) *Monitor your symptoms as they relate to your water intake, then adjust your intake and schedule accordingly.*

Can Anxiety Be Organic?

Unfortunately, many people who suffer from anxiety or depression do not realize that their symptoms may be part of an underlying physical disorder. They try several therapies and do not get well. If you are in this group:

> *86) Find out whether your symptoms are the result of a physical disorder.*

Consider getting a thorough medical exam. A persistent state of anxiety may indicate a physical state that is not optimal.

There may be a chemical imbalance in your brain, a sugar-level problem in your blood, a digestive problem, or a problem with your nervous system. If such a problem is found, a doctor can treat it with drugs, surgery, or lifestyle modification.

Physical problems that may create symptoms of anxiety include the following:

- **Digestive**—gastroesophageal reflux
- **Blood sugar**—low blood sugar (hypoglycemia)

- **Cardiovascular**—angina pectoris, arrhythmia, mitral valve prolapse, congestive heart failure, etc.

- **Respiratory**—hyperventilation, asthma, hypoxia, chronic obstructive lung disease

- **Endocrine**—hyperthyroidism, overactive adrenal glands

- **Drug effects**—steroids, neuroleptics, etc.

- **Neurological**—multiple sclerosis, brain infection, inner ear disease, delirium, head injury

Examinations and laboratory tests will either confirm or exclude any conditions that are known to create anxiety symptoms. Undergoing a physical examination may help you see your anxiety as a physical (and possibly treatable) problem rather than a personality issue.

Section 5

❧

The Higher Road to Reducing Anxiety

Practice Spirituality

Spirituality has an undeniable place in the treatment of anxiety. Scientists are now studying the roles of prayer, meditation, and devotion in treating problems of the mind.

If you are religious or are open to religion-based treatments of anxiety, consider spiritual approaches. They are used by faith-oriented social services and various church support groups, but some therapists also use them.

Here are some ways that spirituality can help in the treatment of anxiety:

87) *See the larger view.*

Spirituality offers a framework for viewing life from a larger perspective. It helps you to see the big picture, which may put your anxiety into perspective and even give meaning to how you deal with it.

88) *Be aware that, against a larger worldview, the small things tend to find their own places.*

When we see things in their proper perspectives, we are less anxious.

89) *Know that anxiety itself is part of the growth process.*

It often means there are deep personal issues that need (or even want) to be dealt with.

90) *Understand that many things happen for a reason.*

It is not always helpful to try to control them.

Spirituality finds a place for anxiety. It is not as quick as medicine to try to "cure" it. Often, anxiety is a sign that there is something in the psyche moving toward maturation, but encountering resistance. If you have a religious bent and a desire to explore this, a minister, rabbi, or a meditation teacher may be able to help you.

You can be an atheist and still practice spirituality. In fact, many scientists, through studying the world around them, have arrived at worldviews very similar to those of religion, but without the dogma. Faiths like Buddhism and Taoism do not deal with a god *per se*. You can also practice various forms of meditation without a religious bent. Mindfulness meditation, for example, does not require a belief-oriented framework. Also, reason and logic can expand or sharpen a spiritual outlook. Most bookstores offer books on spirituality—ask a salesperson for help finding one. Libraries may be of great assistance as well.

Learn the Art of Mindfulness

Mindfulness is usually associated with religious practice, but at its core, it is merely the intensive training of the attention span to watch mental and physical states as they occur. A practitioner focuses attention on the mind and body and watches these mental and physical states rise and fall. The benefit of successful mindfulness is its ability to help you break unhealthy patterns. Scientists are discovering that meditation can treat a variety of ailments, from pain to depression to anxiety. Therefore:

91) Learn the art of mindfulness.

Mindfulness helps a person recognize anxiety: when it occurs, when it does not occur, what makes it arise, what makes it worse, and what makes it go away. Eventually, this insight can lessen anxiety because it removes the conditions that create it. Also, it can give the person control over his/her mind and body.

In some people, mindfulness can also arouse anxiety. This may happen if repressed or unacceptable thoughts come to the surface of consciousness. If mindfulness practice makes you uneasy but you still want to try it, consider consulting a therapist or a meditation center.

Often, the guide there will be skilled in recognizing and dealing with these phenomena. But for most people, anxiety will not surface.

A typical mindfulness training session will consist of any of the following:

- Watching the breath as you inhale and exhale

- Becoming aware of body parts during movement

- Becoming aware of thoughts and feelings as they arise, occur, and go away

Many churches, universities, and hospitals now offer short courses in mindfulness meditation, and the number of such offerings is growing rapidly.

Quote

My career counselor told me to write down my errors when I made them so I would have something concrete to look at, and even to create a tracking system so I could see how my error rate fluctuated and also so I could more easily learn from my mistakes rather than run from them. So instead of trying to CONTROL my emotions, I just wrote down what happened.

By writing down my errors when they happened, I was better able to notice what kinds of things might trigger this "transference" to start happening. Now, when I make a mistake that might start the paranoid spiral, I notice it much faster and can "nip it in the bud" through positive self-talk and taking physical breaks.

Amy
Columbus, Ohio

Face Your Phobias

92) *The only tried and true way to defeat a phobia is to face it head-on.*

All else is merely a way of lessening its symptoms.

If you have a phobia, chances are you frequently think about confronting it. You dream of confronting it. Sufferers frequently *want* to do exactly what their fear keeps them from doing; some were proficient at it in years past. They know more than anyone how irrational the fear is.

In therapy, you won't be exposed to your fear all at once (unless you request it). Instead, you will undergo what is called "exposure therapy." Exposure involves recreating the anxiety gradually, but pairing it with a situation that is not anxiety-producing. Eventually, you will no longer associate the fear with the feared thing.

How exposure therapy works

In exposure therapy, you face your fear gradually. If you have a fear of spiders, for example, you will do a series of steps such as the following:

- Talk about them with your therapist.

- Look at pictures of them.
- Look at a dead one several feet away.
- Look at a live one up close.
- Perhaps let a live spider crawl on your skin.

Remember that exposure may take weeks or months. Relapses can make the fear stronger, so you must be committed to the therapy.

A good book on anxiety therapy will detail steps for many phobias. There are also steps for post-traumatic stress disorder, panic attacks, and obsessive-compulsive disorder. If you have generalized anxiety instead of a phobia, then use many of the other tips mentioned in this book on a gradual basis.

Get Connected

One of the traits common among those with anxiety is isolation. The isolation may contribute to the anxiety or vice versa, but usually they feed each other. Social connections often reduce the pains of anxiety, especially if they become a regular part of life. Some people meet their needs for social activity through the Internet. Although this may be a good start for some people, it may ultimately reinforce isolationist tendencies.

Getting connected is about more than just being social. It means creating relationships that double as coping mechanisms. These coping mechanisms may keep generalized anxiety under control. In fact, scientists are learning that social interaction influences brain development for the better.

Human beings are social creatures by nature, so it isn't surprising that isolation triggers many of the emotional and cognitive symptoms of anxiety. People vary, however, and if you are not naturally social, this chapter may not apply to you.

What can you do to get connected?

93) *Volunteer. Find something you are passionate about and volunteer for activities that use it. Passion is itself an antidote to anxiety.*

This is true because of the rule that anxiety cannot occur simultaneously with

> **Tip**
>
> Getting and staying connected to larger social groups carries the added benefit of teaching you how others combat their own anxieties.

strong feelings/emotions. For some, anxiety is a neurotic substitute for genuine passion.

Your local social service organizations can help you find placements. If you have anxieties about money and/or work, volunteering may help you challenge them.

94) *Take a class. Not only will you make new connections, but often you will meet others seeking social connections.*

95) *If you are in school, join a study group or a society that is connected to your major.*

96) *If you shy away from group activities, just say hello to more people. You may create acquaintances that evolve pressure-free into friendships.*

97) *Those with severe social anxiety may benefit from trying connection therapies under professional care.*

Feel Your Pain

Anxiety is a normal and healthy part of life, as long as it does not develop into a disorder. Many anxiety-prone people often have an obsessive need to be in control: of their feelings, of others' feelings, of events, and of their own and others' behavior. They crave predictability. When things happen unexpectedly, anxiety sufferers begin to experience their symptoms. If you are one of these people, you may benefit from giving up control over events, people, and even your own reactions to events. Spiritual people see it as letting God or something like God direct the action.

You may have noticed that when you try to control your anxiety symptoms, they get worse. A solution to this predicament is to simply let yourself feel those symptoms. Do this little by little so the process is manageable. By giving up control gradually, you create a situation where anxiety becomes unnecessary.

98) *Understand that you can't control everything.*

Several factors go into forming any event.

99) *Understand that things often happen for reasons that are beyond your influence, control, or understanding.*

100) *See occasional failure realistically.*

Occasional failures mean that you succeed most of the time.

101) *Take relapses in stride.*

You may have been trying to do too much too fast, or you may have been expecting too much progress too soon; or, perhaps you need a new approach.

102) *Watch your anxiousness in any triggering situations. It may be telling you to make certain changes.*

103) *Remember that unexpected outcomes might be more favorable to you than outcomes that you had wanted.*

104) *When mild or moderate anxiety arises, let yourself feel it. It won't kill you.*

Something to remember

Anxiety is physiologically the same as excitement. The two differ only in how they are interpreted by you. With practice, you may learn to view certain anxiety-provoking events as exciting ones instead.

Join an Anxiety Support Group

Misery does indeed love company. How else to account for the popularity of therapy support groups? Knowing that others have the same symptoms makes your own more manageable.

> 105) *Check your nearest hospitals for support groups for anxiety sufferers.*

Therapy groups abound in clinics and hospitals and exist for those who have depression, various addictions, or any of a variety of mental afflictions.

> 106) *Look for a therapy group at church.*

> 107) *There are even online support groups that use message boards and chat rooms. These are especially good starting points for people with social phobia to begin addressing their problems.*

What goes on in an anxiety support group?

Many groups are run by a psychiatrist or other therapist. This person helps direct therapeutic activities. Here is a partial list of things you might do in one of these settings:

- Discuss symptoms.
- Explore possible reasons why the anxiety or phobia exists.
- Share coping strategies.
- Help each other with "homework" that is designed to identify and treat anxiety situations.
- Form a support network for your out-of-group times.

Quote

When I went to my first social anxiety support group, I saw signs in the hallway every ten feet or so to guide us. This kept our phobia at bay for the time being. Once in the therapy room, none of us spoke to each other. But just giving my name to the group was a great victory for me. After three months, I was able to give a short speech to the group. From there, I graduated to my college Toastmasters, where I began to tackle my social phobia with greater ease.

MG
Madison, Wisconsin

Use Anxiety to Your Benefit

In some situations, anxiety is a good thing and should be encouraged. It can motivate you to take action on something you would otherwise hesitate to do. It can push you to do what you have been neglecting or postponing. Some people have used test anxiety to study harder. Others have used "time anxiety" to better organize their lives. Still others have harnessed anxiety about money to learn how to save money. Successful people *use* anxiety; they do not let anxiety use them.

Consider using your anxieties in constructive ways. As long as you can control it, you can use it for good. In fact, anxiety often goes hand in hand with creativity, sensitivity, and high intelligence. When used well, anxiety is less troublesome.

108) *List everything about which you are anxious, obsessive, or phobic. Then find a use for each one, whether as a career, hobby, or life enhancement. Use the list started below or develop your own.*

If you are:	Try
Anxious about proper communication	A job as an editor
Anxious about money	A job as a financial planner
Anxious about order	Interior decorating
Anxious about life	Journaling, fiction writing, acting, etc.

Remember: Don't let anxiety take over. If it does, you will not do well in your pursuits. For example, if you are a financial planner, you may feel tempted to steer your clients into too many risk-averse investments. There is a healthy range of anxiety, and your goal is to stay within it.

Get Professional Help

When all else fails, many of us head for the doctor's office. Going for help is itself an attack on anxiety, since it requires strong willpower and confidence, two qualities that help defeat anxiety disorders.

The doctor will ask about your symptoms, how long you have experienced them, which ones are the worst, and whether a particular event triggered them. You will discuss which treatments appeal to you. Knowing your history will make this easier. For example, if you were fine until a particular event took place many years ago, then the therapist may suggest hypnosis. Or, an anxiety filled with unhealthy thinking patterns may require a cognitive approach that teaches realistic ones.

There are several approaches to treating anxiety. Some doctors will overlap them. Try each of these for a fit.

109) **Cognitive**. *This approach deals with how thinking patterns create mental states.*

110) **Psychoanalytic**. *This approach, made famous by Sigmund Freud, looks at how your early experiences shaped your mind and biological drives.*

111) **Behavioral**. *The behavioral outlook is concerned with conditioning and learning. Therapy involves pairing the trigger of the anxiety with something that is by nature non-anxiety-forming, such as happiness or relaxation. Anxiety is not compatible with strong emotional states.*

112) **Phenomenological/spiritual**. *This semi-religious method covers anxiety as it fits into the "big picture" of existence. It often sees a place for anxiety. It may be appropriate for those with religious propensities. Carl Jung and Abraham Maslow were influential in this field.*

113) **Medical/physiological**. *This approach deals with the biology of anxiety. It uses pharmaceuticals for treatment, but may overlap with the other approaches.*

Where to go for help?

Try a social service agency, a hospital, or a mental health facility. If they do not offer therapeutic services, they will usually know where you can find them. If cost is a problem, universities and various social services often provide low-cost therapy.

114) *Consult national or statewide organizations that address anxiety. Here are just a few well-known ones:*

A. *Anxiety Disorders Association of America (www.adaa.org)*

B. Anxiety Panic Internet Resource (www.algy.com/anxiety)
C. National Anxiety Foundation (http://www.lexington-on-line.com/naf.html)
D. Social Phobia/Social Anxiety Association (http://www.socialphobia.org/)
E. Freedom from Fear (http://www.freedomfromfear.org/)
F. National Institute of Mental Health (http://www.nimh.nih.gov/healthinformation/anxietymenu.cfm)

Create a Plan to Combat Anxiety

115) Create a detailed, focused plan to tackle your anxiety.

Now you are ready to deal with your anxiety. This last step is the longest and most challenging, and it involves taking stock of all your symptoms and issues, then finding an approach to treat them. The ideas presented here will help you reduce your anxiety symptoms and live a freer life. Review the previous chapters and select the ideas that resonated with you the most. Those are the areas that will offer you the greatest help.

Use the chart below to help you. It will take a while to gather all your symptoms. You may want to create a larger chart and put it somewhere you'll see it frequently. Consider making a wallet-sized version to carry around, also, to capture ideas that will pop into your head when you least expect them.

Remember: By addressing your symptoms a little bit each day, you will regain more control of your life. With anxiety treatment, slow and steady wins the race. A few ideas have been started for you below. Good luck!

Anxiety Problem	Treatment Approach
Fear of speaking in public	See therapist for exposure therapy.
Anxiousness in midday	Drink adequate water, eat healthy diet, avoid sugar.
Unexplained anxiety symptoms	Get a medical exam to rule out organic causes.

Appendix

Reference List of 115 Ways to Reduce Anxiety

1) Know the difference between an anxiety disorder and regular anxiety.

2) To design an effective treatment plan, you need to know which type of anxiety you have.

3) Narrow your anxiety down to the correct number of types, as this will help to reduce it. This works because once you know the extent of your anxiety, you feel in control of a larger part of your mental universe.

4) Prove that you have anxiety or fear.

5) Write down all your fears.

6) Find specific examples of things that are falling apart in your life. Then make a list of things that are *not* falling apart.

7) Speak in different scenarios, such as on the phone, in a supervisor's office, etc. Learn that not all social situations provoke anxiety.

8) Break up tasks into parts. Then see whether you can do them.

9) See anxiety as a natural part of life.

10) Do not see yourself as a victim.

11) Think "I failed in this one attempt. I will try it another way. Maybe another way will work."

12) Think "I have anxiety in only certain areas of my life, not in all of them."

13) Think "Certain areas of my self aren't working well, such as self-esteem and social functioning."

14) Think "High expectations do not work at all times."

15) Try "gray" thinking instead. This thinking is realistic because it takes the nuances of experience into account.

16) Think "I have low self-esteem in certain areas only."

17) Think "There are several right ways to do things."

18) Think "Even intelligent people can do stupid things."

19) Think "Most things can work with imperfections in them," or "Perfection takes time."

20) Examine beliefs that may be creating or worsening anxiety.

21) Identify thinking patterns you thought you believed in but really didn't.

22) Examine anxiety-causing beliefs that do have a basis in reality.

23) Watch for certain philosophical themes that jump out at you.

24) Take a course in logic.

25) Look for the beauty in imperfect things.

26) Note all your small successes. Write them down in a journal.

27) Add up all the tasks you have put off doing for perfectionistic reasons.

28) Deliberately do some things imperfectly, just so you can monitor how you feel about them.

29) Break up long tasks into small ones that do not provoke any perfectionistic anxiety.

30) Practice active awareness on how your perfectionistic thinking arises, occurs, and goes away.

31) Stop thinking, "Such and such went well, but ..."

32) Learn to do things for your own benefit.

33) Find out the motivations behind other people's criticisms of you.

34) Recognize that other people's approval can be valuable but cannot be the basis of your happiness.

35) Take an inventory of all your strengths and develop them.

36) Learn that your self-worth is never dependent on what you do, but who you are as a person.

37) Identify exactly what you really want/need, down to the detail.

38) During confrontation, describe the problem situation to the other person.

39) During confrontation, state how you feel. Be descriptive.

40) State the effect that someone's negative behavior is having on you.

41) During confrontation, state what you want.

42) Use "I" statements to put the focus on what you want: e.g., "I need you to clean up this mess."

43) Avoid attacking the other person's character.

44) Use specifics instead of sweeping generalizations.

45) Examine how insistent you are that you are "cool," "neutral," or "in control."

46) Identify any strong physical symptoms that occur when you are having negative thoughts. They may be a clue that what you are truly feeling is not being expressed or felt.

47) Notice the way people react to you. Their reactions can pinpoint what you are feeling.

48) Start expressing emotions with people you are comfortable with.

49) You may also want to consult a therapist who specializes in emotional therapy.

50) Learn a martial art.

51) Make room for repetitive activities in your life.

52) Walk every day, usually on the same route.

53) Bike or walk to and from work every day.

54) Knit or sew, or do some other artistic activity, even if it's something easy, like paint by number.

55) Do some chore, such as dishes, on a regular basis.

56) Do aerobic exercise.

57) Take up weight training.

58) Learn tai chi.

59) Learn dancing.

60) Try water exercise.

61) Learn natural breathing.

62) Learn deep breathing.

63) Acclimate yourself to the sounds of nature. These sounds have rhythms that contribute to a reduction in anxiety symptoms.

64) Get plenty of sunlight every day, provided you are not restricted for medical reasons.

65) Learn how to get dirty!

66) Get involved in community gardening. For a small yearly fee, you can have access to a plot of land all your own.

67) Volunteer with a state, national, or county park to do outdoor tasks.

68) Do landscaping or other outdoor work for a volunteer agency.

69) Eat foods that contain several nutrients in one.

70) Substitute traditional foods with similar, but nutrient-packed, foods (like spinach for lettuce).

71) Get your nutrients in their natural state.

72) Work on making a regular practice of eating well.

73) Substitute whole-grain alternatives for your white breads, rice, and pastas.

74) Reduce your caffeine intake for a few weeks to see whether it works for you.

75) Drink green tea or chamomile tea. Chamomile is a known reducer of anxiety symptoms.

76) Eat whole-grain cereals.

77) Pair sugary drinks with a protein source, like peanuts.*

78) Eat whole-grain chips. These products improve in quality every year.

79) Try anxiety-reducing herbs, as teas, baths, tinctures, lotions, and/or capsules.

80) Get most of your water early in the day.

81) If you can't get most of your water early in the day, try getting into the habit of drinking a glass of water for each meal.

82) Cut down on alcohol. The resulting dehydration may trigger your symptoms.

83) Eat foods that naturally contain a lot of water.

84) Keep water in your car, at your desk, in your locker, in your backpack, and in other places.

85) Monitor your symptoms as they relate to your water intake, then adjust your intake and schedule accordingly.

86) Find out whether your symptoms are the result of a physical disorder.

87) See the larger view.

88) Be aware that, against a larger worldview, the small things tend to find their own places.

89) Know that anxiety itself is part of the growth process.

90) Understand that many things happen for a reason.

91) Learn the art of mindfulness.

92) The only tried and true way to defeat a phobia is to face it head-on.

93) Volunteer. Find something you are passionate about and volunteer for activities that focus on it. Passion is itself an antidote to anxiety.

94) Take a class. Not only will you make new connections, but often you will meet others seeking social connections.

95) If you are in school, join a study group or a society that is connected to your major.

96) If you shy away from group activities, just say hello to more people. You may create acquaintances that evolve pressure-free into friendships.

97) Those with severe social anxiety may benefit from trying connection therapies under professional care.

98) Understand that you can't control everything.

99) Understand that things often happen for reasons that are beyond your influence, control, or understanding.

100) See occasional failure realistically.

101) Take relapses in stride.

102) Watch your anxiousness in any triggering situations. It may be telling you to make certain changes.

103) Remember that unexpected outcomes might be more favorable to you than outcomes that you had wanted.

104) When mild or moderate anxiety arises, let yourself feel it. It won't kill you.

105) Check your nearest hospitals for support groups for anxiety sufferers.

106) Look for a therapy group at church.

107) There are even online support groups that use message boards and chat rooms. These are especially good starting points for people with social phobia to begin addressing their problems.

108) List everything about which you are anxious, obsessive, or phobic. Then find a use for each one, whether as a career, hobby, or life enhancement. Use the list started below or develop your own.

109) **Cognitive**. This approach deals with how thinking patterns create mental states.

110) **Psychoanalytic**. This approach, made famous by Sigmund Freud, looks at how your early experiences shaped your mind and biological drives.

111) **Behavioral**. The behavioral outlook is concerned with conditioning and learning. Therapy involves pairing the trigger of the anxiety with something that is by nature non-anxiety-forming, such as happiness or relaxation. Anxiety is not compatible with strong emotional states.

112) **Phenomenological/spiritual**. This semi-religious method covers anxiety as it fits into the "big picture" of existence. It often sees a place for anxiety. It may be appropriate for those with religious propensities. Carl Jung and Abraham Maslow were influential in this field.

113) **Medical/physiological**. This approach deals with the biology of anxiety. It uses pharmaceuticals for treatment, but may overlap with the other approaches.

114) Consult national or statewide organizations that address anxiety. Here are just a few well-known ones:

A. Anxiety Disorders Association of America (*www.adaa.org*)

B. Anxiety Panic Internet Resource (*www.algy.com/anxiety*)

C. National Anxiety Foundation (*www.lexington-on-line.com/naf.html*)

D. Social Phobia/Social Anxiety Association
   (*www.socialphobia.org*)

E. Freedom from Fear
   (*www.freedomfromfear.org*)

F. National Institute of Mental Health
   (*www.nimh.nih.gov/healthinformation/*

   anxietymenu.cfm)

115) Create a detailed, focused plan to tackle your anxiety.

Notes

Printed in the United Kingdom by
Lightning Source UK Ltd., Milton Keynes
139556UK00001B/65/A